TALKING ABOUT
Smoking

Bruce Sanders

Franklin Watts
London • Sydney

PAPERBACK EDITION PRINTED 2007

© Aladdin Books Ltd 2003

Designed and produced by
Aladdin Books Ltd
2/3 Fitzroy Mews
London W1T 6DF

First published in 2003 by
Franklin Watts
338 Euston Road
London NW1 3BH

Franklin Watts Australia
Level 17/207 Kent Street
Sydney NSW 2000

Franklin Watts is a division of
Hachette Children's Books

ISBN: 978 0 7496 7759 6

Design: Flick, Book Design
and Graphics

Picture research:
Brian Hunter Smart

A CIP record for this
book is available from
the British Library.

Dewey Classification:
362.29'6

Printed in Malaysia

The consultant, Dr. Hilary
Pinnock, is a principal in
general practice at Whitstable
Health Centre, and GPIAG
Clinical Research Fellow in
the Department of General
Practice and Primary Care,
University of Aberdeen.

The publishers would like
to acknowledge that the
photographs reproduced in
this book have been posed
by models or have been
obtained from photographic
agencies.

Contents

"What does smoking have to do with me?"

We live in a world where people can choose whether or not to smoke. You might know somebody at home or in your school who does. This is their choice. As you grow up, you have the chance to make up your own mind about smoking. Remember, it's your choice.

If your parents smoke it can seem a normal thing to do – but most adults don't smoke.

This book will help you to decide for yourself. It explains why people start smoking, how smoking makes them feel and how it affects their health.

If you are tempted to try smoking, talk about it with friends first. There's no need to do something just because other people around you are doing it.

"Where does smoking come from?"

People in the Americas have chewed or smoked tobacco for thousands of years. When Europeans first arrived there, about 500 years ago, local people gave dried tobacco leaves as a gift. Soon after, tobacco was being grown all over Europe. As well as smoking pipes, men started to sniff tobacco powder, called snuff.

Whether it is smoked or chewed, tobacco is harmful to people's health.

Later, it became the fashion to smoke cigars. Then, about 100 years ago, smoking also became popular with women. Cigarettes became the popular way of smoking tobacco, and they remain so today.

Today, one in every three adults smokes. That's over a billion smokers worldwide!

Did you know...

People did not understand that smoking could cause deadly diseases until about 50 years ago. Today, scientists are finding out more and more about the health risks of smoking. Even pets can suffer skin and breathing problems if their owners are regular smokers.

"What is a cigarette?"

Cigarettes are made from tobacco leaves which have been dried, chopped and rolled up in a paper case. Certain chemicals are added which strengthen the feeling of smoking. When a smoker sucks on a cigarette, they may inhale the smoke into their lungs. From the lungs, the chemicals in the smoke enter the bloodstream and the smoker feels the "buzz" that they cause.

Tobacco smoke is mainly:

• **Tar** – a black, sticky substance that carries harmful chemicals to your lungs.

• **Nicotine** – the drug that makes cigarettes so addictive: it makes your body want more.

• **Carbon monoxide** – a poisonous gas that makes it harder for your blood to carry oxygen to your heart and lungs.

Did you know…

Many cigarettes have a filter which removes some tar and nicotine. But there are also small amounts of other harmful chemicals in cigarettes:

• Acetone – used in paint stripper
• Arsenic – used in ant poison
• Butane – used in lighter fuel
• DDT – used in insect poison
• Hydrogen cyanide – poison gas

Some cigarettes are made with a lower tar and nicotine content. But smokers often inhale deeper on these to get the same "buzz".

"What does it feel like to smoke?"

The powerful chemicals in cigarettes act like drugs and can make a smoker feel more lively or awake. The chemicals work fast, so a smoker feels the effect within 10 seconds of their first puff. This feeling, or "buzz", that results from smoking is why some people enjoy cigarettes and get used to them.

The "buzz" from smoking a cigarette doesn't last. Smokers soon want another cigarette.

Smoking relaxes some people. If teenagers are having problems at school or at home, they may turn to smoking to help them cope with stress.

However, needing a cigarette can also make smokers tense or irritable.

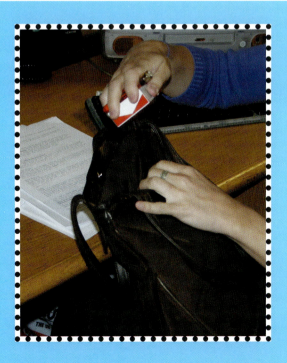

Did you know...

Once people get used to smoking, it soon becomes a habit. They get used to the feeling of a cigarette in their hand or carrying cigarettes around. But smoking is more than just a habit. The chemicals in cigarettes make smokers want one cigarette after another. This is known as "addiction".

"Why is smoking bad for you?"

Giving up smoking can reduce the risk from many deadly diseases.

Smoking is harmful because:
① It badly damages your blood vessels. This prevents blood being carried to your heart muscle, which can cause chest pain or a heart attack.

② It affects the flow of blood to the brain, which can cause a stroke.
③ Cigarette smoke destroys lung tissue, making it hard to breathe air in and out.

As a result, smokers are more likely to die young: from lung cancer, from heart disease or from a heart attack. They are also more likely to suffer from illnesses affecting the lungs and breathing, such as emphysema and asthma.

Women who smoke when they are pregnant can also damage their baby's health.

Think about it

Smoking causes 4 million deaths every year. That's four times the number caused by drugs, alcohol and traffic accidents combined. In fact, someone dies from a smoking-related disease every 8 seconds. If it has taken you 30 minutes to read this far, then over 220 people have died from smoking since you started reading.

"How does smoking harm other people?"

When someone smokes a cigarette, they breathe in just 15 per cent of the smoke. The rest of the smoke goes into the air and is often breathed in by other people. Inhaling the smoke produced by other people's cigarettes is known as passive smoking and can be equally as harmful as smoking cigarettes directly.

People who smoke may damage the health of people they live and work with.

Being in a smoky room can make you feel dizzy, give you a headache or make you want to cough. It can make people with asthma wheeze.

More seriously, if you regularly breathe in other people's smoke, you are more likely to suffer from the deadly diseases that can result from smoking.

Talk about it

Does one of your family smoke? If they do it when you're around and you don't like it, you should tell them. Even if you don't mind, you should let them know that it can harm you or other members of the family. If they don't agree, you could ask them to talk to a doctor or nurse. They can also find out more on one of the websites on page 31.

"What are the other problems with smoking?"

In the past, adverts made smoking seem glamorous. The reality is very different. When you smoke, your breath, hair and clothes smell of stale tobacco smoke.

Tar from tobacco smoke turns your fingers yellow, stains your teeth and gives you bad breath. Smoking damages your skin and gives even young smokers wrinkles.

People who don't smoke have a lot more money to spend on other things.

Smoking also costs a lot of money. Someone who starts smoking at 18 could spend tens of thousands of pounds on cigarettes during their life.

Think how this money could have been spent on other things, such as food, clothing, holidays or going out with friends and family.

Did you know…

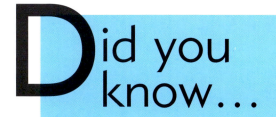

The tobacco industry also affects the environment. Tobacco plants need lots of harmful chemicals to help them grow, which make the land less fertile for other crops.

Large areas of forest are also cut down to provide firewood to dry the tobacco leaves before they are sent to the cigarette factories.

"Why do people start smoking?"

Some young people start smoking because they are curious and want to find out what it is like. They may think that smoking will make them look glamorous or grown-up.

Many smokers say they hated the taste of their first cigarette. But because they saw others enjoying cigarettes, they tried again. In time, they got used to smoking.

Don't let others influence your decisions. Saying "no" to smoking is your choice.

Many people start smoking because their best friend smokes, or because they want to fit into a group. Others find it hard to say "no" when a friend offers them a cigarette.

Young people are also much more likely to start smoking if one of their parents or an elder brother or sister is a smoker.

Think about it

In the past, smoking was made to look cool or exciting through sponsorship of the fashion industry and motor racing. There are now laws banning cigarette advertising in many countries, but smoking is still glamorised in many movies.

"When do people start?"

Some children may think that smoking is a grown-up thing to do because by law you cannot buy cigarettes until you are 16. Yet most grown-ups don't smoke, and few adults take up smoking.

In fact, most smokers start when they are teenagers. Young people may want to rebel against their parents. Smoking is their way of saying, "I'm old enough to do what I want to my body".

Many teenagers know that smoking can harm them, but they find it difficult to imagine that it will make them very ill many years later.

They may say, "I can give up when I'm older", but they don't realise how hard this is.

Some tobacco firms have paid film heroes to smoke their cigarettes so that young people will copy them.

My Story

"My Uncle Dave had been a smoker since he was 14. Then, a couple of weeks after his 40th birthday, the doctor told him he had lung cancer. He couldn't believe it. He'd known about the dangers of smoking, but he never thought it would affect him. He'd felt healthy until recently."

Billy

"Why don't people just stop smoking?"

You may have heard a smoker saying, "I really need a cigarette". That's because the nicotine in tobacco makes their body want more.

As soon as they start to smoke, this drug gets to work very quickly, so the smoker's craving goes away very quickly.

Some people smoke to relax. But there are other ways to relax, such as sports and hobbies.

As soon as a person stops smoking, however, their nicotine level drops and their body wants more of it.

That's why it is so easy to get hooked on cigarettes. People often begin with one or two cigarettes a day.

They smoke more and more until they find it really hard to say "no" to a cigarette.

My story

"Smoking cigarettes made my Gran really ill last year. But even though she knows they could kill her, she just can't stop. She says she enjoys them too much. Now when someone offers me a cigarette, I think about how hard it will be to give them up."
Ade

"Why is it so hard to give up smoking?"

If you know someone who is trying to give up smoking, you will know how hard it is. Nicotine works like a strong drug. When someone stops smoking, their body misses the nicotine. They may get headaches, feel anxious, or find they cannot sleep. This is why they may start smoking again after just a few days.

It is much easier not to start smoking at all than it is to give it up later.

Teenagers do not always feel the bad effects of smoking. But by the time they notice the damage smoking does to their body, it is much harder to stop.

Did you know…

Most adult smokers say that if they were a teenager again, they would choose *not* to smoke. As people grow old, they want to carry on doing the things they enjoy. By not smoking, you've got a much better chance of staying fit and healthy all your life.

"How can smokers quit?"

If people want to give up cigarettes, they need a lot of willpower. It helps to keep thinking about the benefits of stopping: a healthy body, fresh breath and more money in their pocket. They also need help and support from family and friends. If someone you know is trying to give up, let them know you support them.

People who quit smoking find they get out of breath a lot less. That's why sports stars don't smoke.

Cutting down bit by bit doesn't work. After one cigarette, most smokers will want another.

They should choose a day to stop smoking completely, and throw away all their cigarettes and lighters so there is no temptation.

My story

"My Dad is a different person since he quit. For a start, his clothes don't stink and he smells a lot nicer. He's started playing football again and I go to watch the matches. His team isn't much good, but we always have a good run around after the game."
Katie

"What can be done?"

There are more and more places where smoking is banned: on buses, in cinemas, in restaurants and in offices. In some countries, smoking is banned in public places. Not all smokers are happy about this. But many of them agree that if cigarette smoke harms other people, it isn't fair to smoke around them.

If you are not sure where the "no smoking" area is, you can always ask.

Since smoking causes so many deaths, you might think it is a good idea to ban smoking altogether.

But because smoking is so addictive, smokers would find other ways of getting hold of tobacco. Many people also believe that smokers have the right to choose.

Talk about it

Since most people start smoking when they are young, many schools teach about the dangers of smoking. You may have already learnt about it at school or taken part in competitions on national no-smoking day. If not, you could ask your teacher to hold a class discussion about smoking.

What about me?

- If you are tempted to try a cigarette yourself, think about why you want to smoke.

- Everyone likes to try things out as they grow up, but smoking is different. Because of the chemicals in cigarettes, it can be hard to stop smoking once you have started.

- Smoking can seem cool or grown-up, but in the future it could make you very ill, and may even kill you.

- Your friends or an elder brother or sister may offer you cigarettes. Don't ever be forced into smoking by others. Make up your own mind.

Books about smoking

If you want to read more about smoking, try:

Encyclopedia of Smoking and Tobacco by
Arlene Hirschfelder (Greenwood Press)
My Healthy Body - Breathing by
Jen Green (Franklin Watts)
Smoking: Current Controversies by
Auriana Ojeda (Greenhaven Press)

Contact information

If you would like to talk to someone who doesn't
know you, these organisations can help put you
in touch with people trained to help:

Action on Smoking and Health (ASH)
102 Clifton Street
London EC2A 4HW
Tel: 020 7739 5902
Email: action.smoking.health@dial.pippex.com
A public health charity campaigning to reduce
the health problems caused by tobacco.

QUIT Helpline
Tel: 0800 00 22 00
Email: stopsmoking@quit.org.uk.
An independent charity whose aim is to save lives
by helping smokers to stop.

On the Web

These websites are also helpful:

www.ash.org.uk, www.ashaust.org.au
www.givingupsmoking.co.uk
www.quit.org.uk, www.quit.org.au
www.smokefreekids.com
www.tobaccofreekids.org

NHS Smoking Helpline
Tel: 0800 169 0 169
A helpline for smokers
who want to quit.

ASH, Australia
PO Box 572
Kings Cross
NSW 1340
Tel: 02 93341876
A charity campaigning to
reduce the health problems
caused by tobacco.

Quitline, Australia
Tel: 131 848
The Quitline is a telephone service to help
smokers who want to quit.

There is lots of useful information about smoking on the internet.

Index

Photocredits

Abbreviations: l-left, r-right, b-bottom, t-top, c-centre, m-middle
All photos supplied by PBD except for:
3tr, 3mr, 7tr, 17tr, 20b, 18m, 19b — Corbis. 3br, 12b, 13r — Image State. 4b, 27b —Digital Vision.
5b, 16b, 24b, 29b — Roger Vlitos. 6b, 15br — Corel. 7b — Corbis Royalty Free. 9bl — Digital
Stock. 17bl — Select Pictures. 8b, 21t, 23r — Image 100. 9b, 25b, 26b — Photodisc. 11b — Flick
Smith. 22b — Brand X Pictures.